CHAMPAGNE CHARLIE

This script is published by
DCG Publications.

All inquiries regarding purchase of further scripts and current royalty rates should be addressed to:

DCG Media Group
Vamos 73008
Chania
Crete
Greece

Email: info@dcgmediagroup.com
www.dcgmediagroup.com

Conditions

- All DCG Publication scripts are fully protected by the copyright acts. Under no circumstances must they be reproduced by photo-copying or any other means, either in whole or in part.

- The license to perform referred to above only relates to live performances of this script. A separate license is required for video-taping or sound recording, which will be issued on receipt of the appropriate fee.

- The name of the author shall be clearly stated on all publicity, programs etc. The program credits shall state "Script provided by DCG Publications".

CHAMPAGNE CHARLIE

BY

GLYN IDRIS JONES

A
Victorian Music-Hall
Entertainment

Based on the life and songs of
the man who was
"Champagne Charlie"
George Leybourne
1842 - 1884

DCG
Publications

First Published in Greece 2010

© Glyn Idris Jones
The author's moral rights have been asserted

DCG Publications
www.dcgmediagroup.com

ISBN 978-960-98418-7-0

Typeset by
DCG Publications

Printed in England by
Lightning Source.

First Produced
at the

Intimate Theatre
Palmers Green

24th July 1984

Directed by
Glyn Jones

with
Christopher Beeching
as
George Leybourne

Musical Director
Jeff Clarke

This version first performed at the
Little Theatre Hebden Bridge
5th September 1988

with
Christopher Beeching

Paul Knight
Piano

Julian Wightman	Gary Pulleyn
Trumpet / Cornet	Trombone

Christopher Beeching as George Leybourne - 'After the Opera'

Act One

A cloth covered table on which are a period bottle of champagne and a glass on a salver and a wig block. Downstage and to one side an upright piano. Upstage, a large screen.

Upstage, between piano and screen, a wall, decorated with Leybourne song covers, the most prominent of which is MUSIC MAD.

Downstage, below the screen, an easel, on it a blow-up of the CHAMPAGNE CHARLIE song cover.

A barrel organ is heard playing popular Leybourne tunes.

LIGHTS FADE TO BLACKOUT.

In the blackout the PIANIST enters and takes his place. The music segues from TAPE to LIVE.

LIGHT starts to come up on the wall.

Simultaneously there is the sound of a music hall audience, the sound rising to a crescendo.

FLASH – LEYBOURNE appears in front of the wall.

MUSIC MAD.

LEYBOURNE:

SO FOND OF MUSIC I HAVE BEEN...
ITS KNOWLEDGE TO OBTAIN...
THAT LOVE COMBINED WITH MUSIC...
FOLKS SAY HAVE TURNED MY BRAIN....
MY PLAYING ON THE JEW'S HARP...
IT WON SWEET JULIANA...
WHILE I THAT INSTRUMENT WOULD PLAY...
SHE'D VAMP ON HER PIANO...

OH! LOVE AND MUSIC'S SENT ME MAD...

MY FRIENDS ALL SAY IT SERVES ME GLAD...
DO, RE, DO... RE, MI, FA, SOL, DO...
RE, ME, FA, SOL, LA, SI, DO, RE, ME, FA, SOL, LA..
DO, RE, DO... RE, ME, FA, SOL, DO...
RE, MI, FA, SOL, LA, SI, DO, DO, DO, DO.

THINGS WENT ON WELL TILL ONE SAD NIGHT...
AT THE PLACE WHERE SHE WAS PLAYING
A CHEEKY COMIC SINGER CAME....
WHO ATTENTION HER WAS PAYING.
HE SANG THE LOT OF LEYBOURNE'S SONGS...
AND KEPT THE HOUSE IN ROARS...
WHEN SHE THE PREFERENCE GAVE TO HIM...
BECAUSE OF HIS APPLAUSE.

OH! LOVE AND MUSIC'S SENT ME MAD...
MY FRIENDS ALL SAY IT SERVES ME GLAD...
DO, RE, DO... RE, MI, FA, SOL, DO...
RE, ME, FA, SOL, LA, SI, DO, RE, ME, FA, SOL, LA..
DO, RE, DO... RE, ME, FA, SOL, DO...
RE, MI, FA, SOL, LA, SI, DO, DO, DO, DO.

DO, RE, DO... RE, MI, FA, SOL, DO...
RE, ME, FA, SOL, LA, SI, DO, RE, ME, FA, SOL, LA..
DO, RE, DO... RE, ME, FA, SOL, DO...
RE, MI, FA, SOL, LA, SI, DO, DO, DO, DO.

The number ends with a FLASH as LEYBOURNE disappears through the wall.

PIANIST: Ladies and gentlemen...Usually, at this point, there is a magical transformation as a truly magnificent piece of scenery, delicately decorated, controlled by an ingenious machine - a stagehand - and illuminated with brilliant lighting effects, glides slowly towards the back of the stage and, apparently of its own volition, disappears. To be replaced with an extravagant dioramic depiction of the city of Babylon complete with cascading waterfalls, revolving pyramids and, for the first time on any stage, a troop of dancing elephants. Unfortunately the suitcase was abandoned at Crewe so you have had to listen to me whilst the artiste prepares for his next entrance. You will therefore be left forever wondering what you have missed. *(Turn and go. Just before reaching the piano, turn back)* However, under NO CIRCUMSTANCES will there be a refund of your admission. *(Sit)*

LEYBOURNE enters wearing a smoking jacket.

LEYBOURNE: Like my hair? *(He takes off the wig)* You really thought it was mine, didn't you? *(He places the wig on a block)* In London, in the 1860's and '70's false hair was all the rage you know. Oh, yes.... I mean a gentleman could hardly go out not looking like, well... a gentleman. And I don't just mean... *(Indicates the wig)* but.... *(He indicates whiskers)* And.... *(Indicates beard)*... Oh yes, when a lady removed her corsets at night, a gentleman removed his *(Indicates hair)*... and his... *(Moustache)* And his... *(Whiskers)* Surprise surprise. It was all part of being a regular swell. At that time every city clerk and shopkeeper's assistant liked to imagine himself a swell. Swaggering down the Strand with tooth-pick and crutch, a regular brick; a cigar-smoking, game for any spree at night, champagne drinking.... *(He has opened the bottle and now pops the cork and pours out a glass)* swell... cheers! And it was all because of... *(He sips champagne)* ....me. *(He pours a second glass, looks up at the audience)* I'm sorry, you don't know who I am, do you? *(With glasses he crosses over to the pianist. Then, picking out a member of the audience)* Leybourne's the name, madam, George Leybourne. And, if you still don't know who I am, if I'm nothing but a forgotten ghost, let my music speak for me.....

THE MAN ON THE FLYING TRAPEZE

HE'D FLY THROUGH THE AIR WITH THE GREATEST OF EASE,
A DARING YOUNG MAN ON THE FLYING TRAPEZE,
HIS MOVEMENTS WERE GRACEFUL ALL GIRLS HE COULD PLEASE,
AND MY LOVE HE PURLOINED AWAY…

HE'D FLY THROUGH THE AIR WITH THE GREATEST OF EASE,
A DARING YOUNG MAN ON THE FLYING TRAPEZE,
HIS MOVEMENTS WERE GRACEFUL ALL GIRLS HE COULD PLEASE,
AND MY LOVE HE PURLOINED AWAY…

Last time…

HE'D FLY THROUGH THE AIR WITH THE GREATEST OF EASE,
A DARING YOUNG MAN ON THE FLYING TRAPEZE,
HIS MOVEMENTS WERE GRACEFUL ALL GIRLS HE COULD PLEASE,
AND MY LOVE HE PURLOINED AWAY…

END NUMBER.

LEYBOURNE: That song was one of my greatest successes. We Victorians, you know, wrote songs for each and every occasion that took our fancy, and I sang that little number to mark the first appearance in London of the Great Leotard!

CHORD on PIANO.

The man who, it is said, created the flying trapeze. In 1861, at the Alhambra in Leicester Square, he first startled and alarmed his English audience with his daring, dazzling, death-defying aerial display!

PIANIST: Tara!

LEYBOURNE: *(Reacts to PIANIST and then continues)* Later, when trapeze artistes in circus and music hall were two a penny, another took London by storm. This was a young gel who gloried in the name of Lulu! A sylph-like creature whose beauty and virtuosity held her audiences spellbound. Billed as, 'the Beautiful Girl Aerialist and Circassian Catapultist'...

(The PIANIST sniggers)

No; really Circassian Catapultist.... part of her act consisted of being catapulted vertically from the stage to a high trapeze, a distance of twenty five feet! Turning, as she went, a triple somersault! This not only produced gasps from the men....

(PIANIST gasps)

... and shrieks of terror from the ladies....

(PIANIST swoons)

...it also produced letters to the newspapers demanding to know....

PIANIST: *(Recovering and getting to his feet)* Where does the morality lie in forcing this beautiful young gel to literally take her life in her hands in such a fashion in order to earn a crumb... *(He sits)*

LEYBOURNE: And maybe, one day, satisfying the ghoulish expectations of some of her audience by losing her grip and breaking every bone in her lovely young body.

(PIANIST shrieks, covers his eyes, then stands up to get a better view)

PIANIST:	*(Pulling a yukky face)* Ooooh!
LEYBOURNE:	Fortunately it never happened.
PIANIST:	*(Disappointed)* Oh! *(He sits)*
LEYBOURNE:	What happened was even worse.
PIANIST:	Worse?
LEYBOURNE:	Worse.
PIANIST:	*(To audience)* Worse!
LEYBOURNE:	Lulu was courted by any number of admirers, from coronet crowned heads to common cabbies to omnibus cads, all eager to lay their adoring tributes at her dainty feet.
PIANIST:	Yes?
LEYBOURNE:	So when, eventually, it was revealed that Lulu was a lubberly boy....
PIANIST:	A boy! Heavens above! Lulu was a boy?
LEYBOURNE:	Both the moralists and the admirers were... for obvious reasons.... just a little put out.

CRASHING CHORD on the PIANO.

Lulu was also fired from a cannon. And, in the 1880's, another famous female cannonball appeared. This one performed her act at the Royal Aquarium in Westminster and gloried in the name of Zazel.

ZAZEL

ZAZEL, ZAZEL, HAVE YOU SEEN ZAZEL,
ZAZEL, ZAZEL, MY BEAUTIFUL BELLE;

IT'S WONDERFUL FUN WHEN SHE'S SHOT FROM A GUN;
I COULD LIVE AND DIE FOR ZAZEL.

WHATEVER SHE DID SHE SMILED SO NICE,
AS IF IT WERE JOLLY GOOD FUN,
BUT OH MY HEART WENT THUMPITY THUMP,
WHEN I SAW HER GET INSIDE THAT GUN,
AND DIDN'T THE PEOPLE SHOUT, MY EYES!
ALL OVER THE PLACE IT RANG,
WHEN A CHAP HE FIRES THE TOUCH HOLE END,
AND OUT SHE COMES WITH A BANG.

ZAZEL, ZAZEL, HAVE YOU SEEN ZAZEL,
ZAZEL, ZAZEL, MY BEAUTIFUL BELLE;
IT'S WONDERFUL FUN WHEN SHE'S SHOT FROM A GUN;
I COULD LIVE AND DIE FOR ZAZEL.

ZAZEL, ZAZEL, HAVE YOU SEEN ZAZEL,
ZAZEL, ZAZEL, MY BEAUTIFUL BELLE;
IT'S WONDERFUL FUN WHEN SHE'S SHOT FROM A GUN;
I COULD LIVE AND DIE FOR ZAZEL.

END NUMBER.

Once more the moralist came out in force. But their storms of protest only guaranteed a sure-fire hit every time she appeared. Actually there were four Zazels, three on standby, just in case. And though many aerial artistes did fall and break their necks, the Zazels didn't. Neither did Lulu. She... or should I say 'he'?.... eventually retired and emigrated to San Francisco. Leotard didn't retire but died of smallpox at the age of twenty nine. Today you remember Leotard because of the garment worn by dancers to which he gave his name. And now, I hope, you will remember me, because of the songs I sang. If you were to go to the New Year Concert in

Vienna, or hear it being broadcast, you might very well hear this....

THE MOUSETRAP MAN

MOUSETRAPS, MOUSETRAPS, HE'D CRY,
MOUSETRAPS, FINE MOUSETRAPS, WHO'LL BUY?
STRONG AS A HOUSE JUST HAVE ONE AND TRY.
MOUSETRAPS A PENNY, A PENNY WHO'LL BUY?

MOUSETRAPS, MOUSETRAPS, HE'D CRY,
MOUSETRAPS, FINE MOUSETRAPS, WHO'LL BUY?
STRONG AS A HOUSE JUST HAVE ONE AND TRY.
MOUSETRAPS A PENNY, A PENNY WHO'LL BUY?

and

CHAMPAGNE CHARLIE

CHAMPAGNE CHARLIE IS MY NAME,
CHAMPAGNE CHARLIE IS MY NAME,
GOOD FOR ANY GAME AT NIGHT, MY BOYS,
GOOD FOR ANY GAME AT NIGHT, MY BOYS,
CHAMPAGNE CHARLIE IS MY NAME,
CHAMPAGNE CHARLIE IS MY NAME,
GOOD FOR ANY GAME AT NIGHT, BOYS,
WHO'LL COME AND JOIN ME IN A SPREE.

END NUMBER.

I see you turn and look at each other with quizzical glances. "Why?" you ask yourselves, why should a world famous orchestra like the Vienna Philharmonic, and world renowned conductors, fiddle about with such trite trashy stuff? Popular Music! *(He fetches a makeup box)* Well I'll tell you. We Victorians, apart from writing songs for each and every occasion, also liked to take each others songs and arrange them as something else – gallops, quadrilles, marches, waltzes – and, when the great Johann

Strauss came to London to conduct at Covent Garden Opera House, he took a budget of my songs and wrote 'Memories of Covent Garden' especially for his English audience. Listen....

ORCHESTRAL VERSION – MEMORIES OF COVENT GARDEN.
(Leybourne puts on wig, whiskers and make-up)

MUSIC ENDS.

(He stands downstage facing the audience)

You see before you a heavy swell. The heavy swells of the music hall were the Lion Comiques, and there were any number of us. There was the Great Vance, there was Harry Rickards, Walter Laburnam, Jolly John Nash, Harry Liston, The Great MacDermott, Athur Lloyd. But the heaviest swell of them all was .... *(He taps his chest).* And not only the heaviest but the very first to bear the title, 'Lion Comique'. It was a gentleman named J.J.Poole, manager of the Metropolitan Music Hall in the Edgware Road who, on first seeing me perform, was heard to exclaim, 'Why the man is a lion of a comic! A veritable comic lion!' And the label stuck, Frenchified into 'Lion Comique'. Because we Victorians also liked to Frenchify everything. It was chic. So we had... Gymnastique... Pose Plastique.... Characteristique.... Operatique.... Choreographique. It was all rather Eccentrique really. But then I suppose, being French held it's own mystique. And if we weren't Frenchifying everything, we swells were Piccadillyising everything. This.... *(Monocle)* was known as a Piccadilly window. *(He inserts it)* How do you like my Piccadilly window? Quite an eye opener, what? And these.... *(Indicating whiskers)* are Piccadilly weepers.

PIANIST: No actor need fear swallowing his moustache, or whiskers coming off, if he uses Clarkson's Spirit Gum...

(Leybourne holds up the bottle)

PIANIST: Sold only at his wig emporium and repository, 45 Wellington Street, Strand. Sixpence and one shilling a bottle. Sent by post two stamps extra.

LEYBOURNE: That was an advertisement in the Era, a theatrical newspaper of the time. It goes on.

PIANIST: All previous sensation outdone. Clarkson's new mechanical moustache....

LEYBOURNE: Mechanical moustache!

PIANIST: Novelty, simplicity, and grotesque combined. Change in a moment forming three distinct moustaches... without using the hands.

TOGETHER: Without using the hands!!!!

LEYBOURNE: Oh, and didn't we Victorians just love sensation, and novelty, and the grotesque. And the Music Hall gave it all in abundance: comic singers, aerial acrobats, giants and midgets, grotesque dancers, negro delineators, funambulists, grand opera, and Lion Comiques!

(During the above there has been the sound of audience noises, the sound gradually rising in intensity and excitement.)

(At the easel, LEYBOURNE turns back the blow-up of Champagne Charlie to reveal the cover of AFTER THE OPERA. Having done this, he goes behind the screen, the sounds of the audience meanwhile having turned to shouts, cheers, applause, whistles.)

PIANIST: And now, ladies and gentlemen! On behalf

of Messrs Fineberg and Lees, proprietors of the New Star Music Hall, it is with particular pride and particular pleasure, we welcome yet again to our illustrious city of Liverpool, with a complete budget of new songs, the recipient of thunders of applause and shouts of approbation nightly from crowded and enthusiastic audiences wherever he appears, ladies and gentlemen, will you welcome that lion of lion comiques.... Mr George Leybourne!!!!

(LEYBOURNE now appears the other side of the screen wearing the costume shown on the easel)

AFTER THE OPERA

AFTER THE OPERA'S OVER,
GAS TRIES TO OUTSHINE THE STARS,
WHEN HALF OF THE WORLD SLEEPS CONTENTED.
WE'LL DRINK CHAMPAGNE SMOKE FINE CIGARS;
FOR LIFE WITHOUT PLEASURE IS COLD,
AND I SHOULDN'T LIVE VERY LONG,
BUT HOW WE SURVIVE IN THE WEST END.
I'M DELIGHTED TO TELL IN MY SONG.

With a tootle tum tum accompaniment upon the piano we sing....

AFTER THE OPERA'S OVER,
ATTENDING THE LADIES IS DONE,
WE GEMS OF THE VERY FIRST WATER,
COMMENCE WITH OUR FROLIC AND FUN.

I KEEP MY OWN BOX AT THE OPERA,
I'VE RACERS AND HUNTERS AS WELL,
ESTATES AND FINE LANDS IN THE COUNTRY,
SO MUCH MONEY I CANNOT TELL.
THEN WHY SHOULD I LET MYSELF DOWN,
AND NEITHER SPEND MONEY NOR LEND,
FOR MONEY WELL SPENT BRINGS JOYS,
YES MONEY WAS MADE TO SPEND.

AFTER THE OPERA'S OVER,
ATTENDING THE LADIES IS DONE,
WE GEMS OF THE VERY FIRST WATER,
COMMENCE WITH OUR FROLIC AND FUN.

WE GEMS OF THE VERY FIRST WATER,
COMMENCE WITH OUR FROLIC AND FUN.

END NUMBER.

(He stands against the easel and looking at the picture.)

> For life without pleasure is cold,
> And I shouldn't live very long.
>
> Prophetic words....
>
> Would you believe I died three times? The first occasion was in 1876. Late that year I fell very ill, congestion of the lungs. I was in Liverpool at the time and, each week, there was a bulletin in the Entr'acte.

PIANIST: Lying in a critical condition

LEYBOURNE: Then....

PIANIST: Gradually improving.

LEYBOURNE: Then....

PIANIST: Much improved, at home in London.

LEYBOURNE: And then, on December the 2nd, readers were informed that....

PIANIST: The previous Friday it had been commonly reported that Mr George Leybourne was dead.

LEYBOURNE: Of course the paper was delighted to report that

	I was still happily alive but, as the editor, in his grief, had penned a little memoriam, it seemed a pity to waste it and here it was all the same. It read....
PIANIST:	A few lines touching the death of Mr George Leybourne, the celebrated comedian.
LEYBOURNE:	A genial, merry wit has passed away, The mirthful soul, alas, now is no more; Down, down the stream of life one ever gay Has sailed and landed on the other shore...

Can you imagine lying in your sickbed reading that!

The brilliant flame within the lamp of life,
That once so gaily and so brightly shone,
And shed its rays, and banished care and strife,
Has now died out, for he is dead and gone.

The editor of the Entr'Acte was obviously no Lord Tennyson

Yes, dead and gone, I scarce can realise,
That he so full of mirth and fun,
Has passed away forever from our eyes...

And so on and so on. Four years later, blow me down if they didn't kill me off again. This time the death notice was followed up not with a poem but a cartoon.

(He turns back the blow-up to reveal the portrait from the Entr'Acte – THE LATE GEORGE LEYBOURNE)

PIANIST: It is not every comic singer who can enjoy the luxury of reading the announcement of his own death.

LEYBOURNE: I nearly went to law over that one but then I

thought, what's the point? Life is short and hard enough, you need a little touch of luck and you don't need enemies. Anyone in the theatre in those days worked damn hard and, perhaps, the music hall was the hardest of all. Three or four turns a night, each in a different venue that was not uncommon. Sometimes five. And one night I even managed six! It's true! I knew it was Tommy and Joe to a four penny bit you wouldn't believe me but, on 15th of March 1866, I played six halls in four hours. Six halls over an area of twelve miles, and took five or six calls in each. Knocked 'em for six I did. The pet of London they called me. But it was a one off. You couldn't do that every night. Well, you imagine it.... winter... you do your act in a hall stuffily hot from gas jets and bodies, and you're in these togs so you're sweating like a horse, giving your all. Backstage it's freezing, to say nothing of the air outside when you make a dash for your cab. Or the fog's so thick you can't see your hand in front of your face. A quick trot and you're into the next hall; out again, in again; hot, cold, hot, cold. Is it any wonder so many of us died young?

I SAY CABBY

I SAY CABBY, WAITING THERE IN LINE,
WE'LL TROT AWAY FOR I HAVE TO PLAY
ANOTHER HALL BY NINE.
I SAY CABBY, IT'S ON TO YET ONE MORE,
I'M EARNING A BITE SO I'VE BOOKED YOU ALL NIGHT
FROM DOOR TO DOOR.

I SAY CABBY, WHAT WILL BE THE FARE,
TO DRIVE THE EARL ALONG WITH A GIRL,
FROM HERE TO LEICESTER SQUARE,
I SAY CABBY, THE JOB YOU OUGHT TO NAB,
I DO LIKE A RIDE WITH A GIRL BY MY SIDE
IN A HANDSOME CAB.

I SAY CABBY, WHAT WILL BE THE FARE,
TO DRIVE THE EARL ALONG WITH A GIRL,
FROM HERE TO LEICESTER SQUARE,
I SAY CABBY, THE JOB YOU OUGHT TO NAB,
I DO LIKE A RIDE WITH A GIRL BY MY SIDE
IN A HANDSOME CAB.

END NUMBER.

> That song, sung with the greatest success, as we used to say, was written by Joseph Tabrar. A great lad was Joseph. He didn't have much time for other composers though. In fact, no time at all. "Wagner!" he used to say, "Wagner? I could put him to bed and he wouldn't know he'd been alive." And as for the great Sir Arthur Sullivan… well… "Sullivan? Sullivan? I can do all he can do, and more, while you wait, on a bit of old paper the trotters are wrapped in." Joseph wrote hundreds of songs, over a thousand by his own estimation. Though knowing Joseph, maybe he was exaggerating a little. This is probably the one you know best….

DADDY WOULDN'T BUY ME A BOW-WOW

DADDY WOULDN'T BUY ME A BOW-WOW
(BOW-WOW)
DADDY WOULDN'T BUY ME A BOW-WOW
(BOW-WOW)
I HAVE A LITTLE CAT AND I'M VERY FOND OF THAT
BUT I'D RATHER HAVE A BOW-WOW-WOW.

ALL TOGETHER NOW…

DADDY WOULDN'T BUY ME A BOW-WOW
(BOW-WOW)
DADDY WOULDN'T BUY ME A BOW-WOW
(BOW-WOW)
I HAVE A LITTLE CAT AND I'M VERY FOND OF THAT

BUT I'D RATHER HAVE A BOW-WOW-WOW.

END NUMBER.

> Joseph was a plumber and bell hanger by trade, just as I was an engineer before I went on the halls. Well, if you had a trade, it was something to fall back on. Anyway, Joseph was doing a spot of plumbing in the house where I was living at the time and, when he heard who was upstairs, he dashed up amd banged on my door. 'I've got a song,' He says. 'Come in,' says I, 'sit down at the old joanna my boy, and whack on the dominoes.' He did. I bought.

I'M A MILLIONAIRE

I FEEL SO DELIGHTED MY SHIP HAS COME HOME,
MY UNCLE'S RETIRED, NO LONGER TO ROAM,
THE OLD MAN HAS DIED, AND LEFT IN HIS WILL,
THAT ALL IS FOR ME SO I'LL PAY EVERY BILL.
THOUGH I ONCE STUCK IT UP NOW I PAY MONEY DOWN,
AND RIDE IN A CARRIAGE ALL OVER THE TOWN,
I'VE GOT ALL HIS MONEY, HIS DIAMONDS AND PEARLS,
I DON'T CARE WHAT I SPEND SO I'LL TREAT ALL THE GIRLS.

> There you are, take me while I'm in the humour, order of the waiters what you like and I'll pay for it, because...

I'M A DUKE, I'M A LORD, I'M A MAJOR,
SOME DAY I SHALL BE A LORD MAYOR,
I'M AN EARL, I'M A SQUIRE, I'M A CAPTAIN,
IN FACT I'M A MILLIONAIRE.

(He goes into the audience, throwing away fivers)

I'M A DUKE, I'M A LORD, I'M A MAJOR,
SOME DAY I SHALL BE A LORD MAYOR,

I'M AN EARL, I'M A SQUIRE, I'M A CAPTAIN,
IN FACT I'M A MILLIONAIRE.

I'VE GOT FOURTEEN LAWYERS TO SELL UP MY GROUNDS,
BECAUSE I PREFER TO HAVE IT IN POUNDS.
I'VE BOUGHT ALL THE TITLES OF MEN OF GREAT RANK,
I'VE GOT ENOUGH MONEY TO BUY UP A BANK.
A WASHING BILL FOR ONE AND NINE PENCE I HOLD
SO BLESS THE OLD GIRL, I'LL PAY HER IN GOLD.
THOUGH OFTEN I TOLD HER SHE MUST STICK IT UP,
I'LL TREAT HER AND YOU TO A CHAMPAGNE CUP.

I'M A DUKE, I'M A LORD, I'M A MAJOR,
SOME DAY I SHALL BE A LORD MAYOR,
I'M AN EARL, I'M A SQUIRE, I'M A CAPTAIN,
IN FACT I'M A MILLIONAIRE.

(He goes back into the audience on the other side)

I'M A DUKE, I'M A LORD, I'M A MAJOR,
SOME DAY I SHALL BE A LORD MAYOR,
I'M AN EARL, I'M A SQUIRE, I'M A CAPTAIN,
IN FACT I'M A MILLIONAIRE.

(LEYBOURNE back on stage)

> There you are.... fivers, when a fiver was worth a fiver. And for one of you lucky people, worth more than a fiver because you will have won a bottle of champagne! Yes, look on the back. Now who's won? *(Ad lib presentation of Champagne)*

I'M A DUKE, I'M A LORD, I'M A MAJOR,
SOME DAY I SHALL BE A LORD MAYOR,
I'M AN EARL, I'M A SQUIRE, I'M A CAPTAIN,
IN FACT I'M A MILLIONAIRE.

IN FACT I'M A MILLIONAIRE!

END NUMBER.

Joseph wrote one of the last songs I ever sang... *(He sings)...* 'ting ting, that's how the bell goes; ting, ting, a pretty young thing, if you'll be my wife then I'll buy you a ring, and have servants to wait on the ting, ting, ting'... a song set in a teashop. A far cry from champagne. My beginnings too were a far cry from champagne, a working's man cottage near Newcastle, in an area of Gateshead known as Stourbridge, that's where I was born, in 1842, the first of six children. A working man's cottage? Huh! A working man's slum. We Victorians, you know, wrote any number of songs about death, not because death took our fancy, but because we knew all about him. There were plenty of people dying of starvation in our big cities. And diseases that, today, don't mean much, were fatal then... measles, scarletina, gastric fever, and worse... typhoid... typhus... and, in Gateshead.... Cholera! You find that hard to believe? Why? There were no drains. The streets were open sewers encrusted with filth and littered with pigsties, tripe factories, slaughterhouses, where butchers still killed in full view of passers-by. Skinner's yards. My father Joseph was a currier, working with leather. Our drinking water came from the river, the water closet of the whole neighbourhood, and we lived in such terrible overcrowded conditions that people slept on the damp floor, lying so close to each other that every one could touch his neighbour. There were three families living in our tiny cottage. So, after my brother Samuel was born, and remembering the Cholera epidemic of 1831, and fearful of another one threatening, my father moved the whole family to London. There we lived in a tenement block, 67 Nelson Square, Borough, what were called 'Improved dwellings for the working classes.' And right next door lived a little girl named Sarah Ann Fisher. We grew up together, and on the 12th March 1865, I married my Sarah Ann.

LEYBOURNE'S LOVE SONG

LOVE, LOVE, OH WHAT IS LOVE?
LOVE 'TIS THAT MAKES A MAN FEEL SO MUCH RARER,
LOVE LOVE! WHO DOES NOT LOVE,
A MAUDE, A MATILDA, A JANE OR A SARAH?
LOVE IT IS AND LOVE ALONE,
THAT MAKES THE WORLD GO ROUND AND ROUND,
LOVE IS CERTAIN TO BE KNOWN,
WHERE A WOMAN'S TO BE FOUND;
WHEN A FIRST ATTACK YOU'VE GOT
IT'S A KIND OF A SORT OF A DON'T KNOW WHAT.

OH LOVE, BEAUTIFUL LOVE!
LOVE 'TIS THAT MAKES A MAN FEEL SO PECULIAR,
OH, LOVE! BEAUTIFUL LOVE,
A MAN'S BUT A FOOL IF HE FALLS IN LOVE.

OH, LOVE, LUXURIOUS LOVE!
LOVE 'TIS THAT MAKES A MAN FEEL SO PECULIAR,
OH, LOVE! BEAUTIFUL LOVE,
THE WORLD WOULD BE DREARY WERE'T NOT FOR LOVE.

THE WORLD WOULD BE DREARY WERE'T NOT FOR LOVE.

END NUMBER.

After our marriage we moved into lodgings in Islington. We shared them with two other families; a furniture dealer by the name of Hoy, and slate merchants, Maria Gelatly and son. A year later our son, George was born. And eighteen months later, our daughter Florrie. We'd moved again by then. I now had a house of my own, still in Islington, Park Street. A beautiful lass was Florrie, with enormous, dark eyes. She took after me and went on the halls. Always knew she would. The first time she went solo was at the Rosemary Branch in Islington, a really tough little hall, so I went onto the stage to introduce her myself. 'This little girl... this little girl of mine is nervous... give her a chance and she'll make good.' She did. Oh, she never really made the top league, but she was good. Now someone who did make the top league was Jenny Hill. 'The Vital Spark' they called her and she was a tremendous favourite. I remember when she made her first London appearance, at the Pavilion. They wouldn't let her off! This tiny little bag of skin and bones had them eating out of her hands. Call after call while I stood in the wings waiting to go on. What to do? Finally, I marched out on stage, lifted her onto my shoulder, and paraded her. You should have heard the cheers. I thought they were going to take the roof off. Then I marched her off the stage and got on with the act.

OH! THE FAIRIES

THERE'S A YOUNG FRIEND OF MINE WHO IS NEARLY DIVINE,
IF YOU LOOKED IN HIS FACE HE WOULD BLUSH,
IF HE MET A GIRLS' SCHOOL HE'D QUAKE LIKE A FOOL,
AND AWAY FROM THE DARLINGS HE'D RUSH.
ONE NIGHT I SAID 'G' NOW COME OUT WITH ME,
FOR YOU KNOW IT IS NEAR CHRISTMAS TIME,
AND EVERYONE'S GAY, NOW WHAT DO YOU SAY,
IF WE SEE DRURY LANE PANTOMIME...

With the greatest of pleasure, my dear friend, providing we are home in good time. With that, we started off; but when we reached the theatre it was full, not a seat to be had.... Aaaaah! So what should we do but fly to the Alhambra, and secured a seat in the stalls.... Hooray! And when the ballet came on, and the girls were skipping about, my friend awoke like one from a dream and exclaimed...

OH THE FAIRIES, WHOA THE FAIRIES!
NOTHING BUT SPLENDOUR AND FEMININE GENDER,
OH THE FAIRIES, WHOA THE FAIRIES!
OH FOR THE WING OF A FAIRY QUEEN!

OH THE FAIRIES, WHOA THE FAIRIES!
NOTHING BUT SPLENDOUR AND FEMININE GENDER,
OH THE FAIRIES, WHOA THE FAIRIES!
OH FOR THE WING OF A FAIRY QUEEN!

AT LAST WE CAME OUT WITH PAS RATHER STOUT,
AND MAMMAS WITH THEIR DAUGHTERS SO GRAND,
THEN TO THE STAGE DOOR WE WENT, BUT OH LOR,
IT WAS NOTHING LIKE BRIGHT FAIRY LAND....
AND ALL WAS SO COLD, NO SILVER OR GOLD,
THE GIRLS WERE AMISS AND MISNAMED,
MY POOR FRIEND HE GAZED, AND LOOKED ALL AMAZED,
AND THEN ALL AT ONCE HE EXCLAIMED....

OH THE FAIRIES, WHOA THE FAIRIES!
NOTHING BUT SPLENDOUR AND FEMININE GENDER,
OH THE FAIRIES, WHOA THE FAIRIES!
OH FOR THE WING OF A FAIRY QUEEN!

OH THE FAIRIES, WHOA THE FAIRIES!
NOTHING BUT SPLENDOUR AND FEMININE GENDER,
OH THE FAIRIES, WHOA THE FAIRIES!
OH FOR THE WING OF A FAIRY QUEEN!

AND THEN NOT CONTENT, OFF STROLLING WE WENT,
TO THE HAYMARKET'S FAMED SUPPER ROOMS,
AND THERE WE DRANK CHAM', AND CALLED GIRLS REAL JAM,
LIKE YOU HEAR OTHER AWFUL GREAT SPOONS;
BUT WHEN THE PLACED CLOSED, 'SWEET HOME' I

PROPOSED,
AND AWAY FROM THE LADIES DRESSED LOUD,
BUT SOON WE GOT MIXED BETWEEN AND BETWIXT,
AND MY POOR FRIEND I LOST IN THE CROWD.

> Couldn't see him anywhere. But I could hear him... he was shouting out....

OH THE FAIRIES, WHOA THE FAIRIES!
NOTHING BUT SPLENDOUR AND FEMININE GENDER,
OH THE FAIRIES, WHOA THE FAIRIES!
OH FOR THE WING OF A FAIRY QUEEN!

OH THE FAIRIES, WHOA THE FAIRIES!
NOTHING BUT SPLENDOUR AND FEMININE GENDER,
OH THE FAIRIES, WHOA THE FAIRIES!
OH FOR THE WING OF A FAIRY QUEEN!

SO THEN ALL ALONE I MADE MY WAY HOME,
AND QUITE SAFELY I REACHED THE STREET DOOR;
TO BED I SOON CREPT, AND SOUNDLY I SLEPT,
UNTIL I WAS WOKE UP AT FOUR.
MY FRIEND HE ARRIVED WITH SOME FRIENDS ALL ALIVE,
AND WAS LYING HALF DRUNK ON THE STAIRS,
WITH A BOOT IN EACH HAND HE CRIED, 'FAIRY LAND,
AND HANG ALL THE LANDLADIES, WHO CARES?'

OH THE FAIRIES, WHOA THE FAIRIES!
NOTHING BUT SPLENDOUR AND FEMININE GENDER,
OH THE FAIRIES, WHOA THE FAIRIES!
OH FOR THE WING OF A FAIRY QUEEN!

(He goes behind the screen. Returns in fairy costume)

OH THE FAIRIES, WHOA THE FAIRIES!
NOTHING BUT SPLENDOUR AND FEMININE GENDER,
OH THE FAIRIES, WHOA THE FAIRIES!
OH FOR THE WING OF A FAIRY QUEEN!

GIVE ME THE WING OF A FAIRY QUEEN!

END NUMBER.

The wand explodes leaving LEYBOURNE dazed. The PIANIST goes to his assistance and leads him off. As they pass the easel the PIANIST turns over the illustration to reveal another which reads

INTERVAL

He gives the audience a despairing look as they go out.

Christopher Beeching as George Leybourne - 'The Prince of Paradise'

Act Two

The PIANIST enters. He turns back the interval sign to reveal a PORTRAIT of LEYBOURNE. He crosses to the piano, sits, and plays the introduction to the GREAT CHANG POLKA. Then he stands and addresses the audience.

PIANIST: Ladies and gentlemen! With the arrival in these islands from Shanghai and Hong Kong, and with the exhibition at the Egyptian hall of the amazing Fychow giant, Chang Woo Gow, Mr George Leybourne will now dance for you, the Great Chang Polka!

(He sits and plays)

THE GREAT CHANG POLKA

(Through the following section, stilts and Chang costume are removed and put away and LEYBOURNE is now in the costume for THERE'S NOTHING NEW UNDER THE SUN)

LEYBOURNE: How d'you like me stilts? They're nothing. During the skating craze of the seventies I used to perform a number, 'Belle of the Rink' on roller skates. I won't do it for you now. The stage manager forgot to bring them. But there's nothing new under the sun, is there? Oh, you fly around in rockets, but we went up too you know.

UP IN A BALLOON

UP IN A BALLOON, UP IN A BALLOON,
ALL AMONG THE LITTLE STARS SAILING ROUND THE MOON,
UP IN A BALLOON, UP IN A BALLOON,
IT'S SOMETHING AWFULLY JOLLY TO BE UP IN A BALLOON.

UP IN A BALLOON, UP IN A BALLOON,

ALL AMONG THE LITTLE STARS SAILING ROUND THE MOON,
UP IN A BALLOON, UP IN A BALLOON,
IT'S SOMETHING AWFULLY JOLLY TO BE UP IN A BALLOON.

> And you might have nuclear submarines but we went under the sea too....

DOWN IN A DIVING BELL

DOWN IN A DIVING BELL, AT THE BOTTOM OF THE SEA,
THAT'S A PRETTY PLACE THE FISHY SIGHTS TO SEE,
DOWN IN A DIVING BELL, AT THE BOTTOM OF THE SEA,
NICE LITTLE MERMAIDS, PRETTY LITTLE MERMAIDS,
ALL COME COURTING ME.

END NUMBER.

> Traffic tickets? Who doesn't know about traffic tickets? But what's new? My coachman, Sam Carver, was done in Westminster Crown Court in 1872 for reckless driving. Carver by name and carver by nature. Only doing twelve miles an hour he was.

(The PIANIST coughs)

> Well, maybe thirteen... and he was done! Twenty one shillings and costs or fourteen days. I paid up at once of course, but a diabolical liberty I call it. Worried by the younger generation? *(He picks up the paper)* September 23rd 1866.... Youthful crime and our rising generation.... The depravity among the youthful population, male and female, is something fearful to contemplate. Boys practice the vices of the roué and girls just entering their teens possess the knowledge of women and mothers. The immorality among

the juvenile part of the community is one of the most extraordinary phases in the social history of the people. *(He puts down the paper)* See what I mean? And, as for government, there's nothing new there either.

PIANIST: Hear hear!

LEYBOURNE: Mr Gladstone, speaking on the currency, told parliament and the country, 'Monetary theories have driven more men mad than violent grief, violent love, or any other common cause I know of.'

THERE'S NOTHING NEW UNDER THE SUN

THIS WORLD OF OURS GOES ROUND AND ROUND,
THE SAME THING OVER AGAIN,
THE SUN COMES UP AND THE SUN GOES DOWN,
THE SAME SUN OVER AGAIN,
AND UNDER THAT SUN THERE IS NOTHING NEW 'TIS SAID,
AND SO I HAVE FOUND IT TRUE,
THIS LIFE OF OURS 'TWEEN ME AND YOU,
IS THE SAME THING OVER AGAIN.

'TIS THE SAME THING OVER AGAIN,
THE SAME THING OVER AGAIN,
AS THE WORLD GOES ROUND IT WILL SURELY BE FOUND
THE SAME THING OVER AGAIN.

'TIS THE SAME THING OVER AGAIN,
THE SAME THING OVER AGAIN,
AS THE WORLD GOES ROUND IT WILL SURELY BE FOUND
THE SAME THING OVER AGAIN.

END NUMBER.

No, nothing changes. And humans beings will

always be the same. Always their fads and fancies, their loves and hates, their foibles and failures; disappointment hopes and dreams...

THE PRINCE OF PARADISE

AS I DOZED IN MY CHAIR AFTER DINNER ONE DAY,
A FAIRY I SEEMED TO SEE,
WHO SAID, 'MORTAL IF NOT CONTENT WITH YOUR LOT,
SAY, WHAT WOULD YOU LIKE TO BE?'
SO I THOUGHT WITH SUCH A GLORIOUS CHANCE,
I'D GO IN FOR SOMETHING NICE,
SO I MODESTLY DESIRED TO BE,
THE PRINCE OF PARADISE!

AND I WAS THE PRINCE OF PARADISE,
I WAS THE PRINCE OF PARADISE,
EVERY ONE LOVELY, EVERY THING NICE,
JUST THE PLACE FOR ME, DEAR BOYS.
AND I WAS THE PRINCE OF PARADISE,
I WAS THE PRINCE OF PARADISE,
EVERY ONE LOVELY, EVERY THING NICE,
JUST THE PLACE FOR ME.

MUSIC seques into HIT HIM ON THE BOKO

THE SPORT THEY CALL THE FANCY WAS A NOVELTY TO ME,
AND SO THE FAMOUS FIGHT LAST WEEK I THOUGHT I'D GO AND SEE,
I HEARD SOME BOXING LINGO THERE I'D NEVER HEARD BEFORE,
WHEN THE BOXER STEPPED INTO THE RING THE CROWD BEGAN TO ROAR...

At the end of each line of the preceding verse LEYBOURNE walks behind the screen and appears on the other side without first his jacket, then waistcoat, shirt & tie, then his trousers, being dressed only in tights and a sash for the rest of the song.

HIT HIM ON THE BOKO, DOT HIM ON THE SNITCH,
WHAT A PRETTY FIGHTER, WAS THERE EVER SICH?
NAFF HIM ON THE KISSER, CLOCK HIM ON THE DIAL,
SOCK HIM IN THE PEEPERS, CULLY THAT'S THE STYLE!

IT'S GOOD TO WATCH A MILL BETWEEN TWO CHAMPION PUGILISTS,
THEY'RE HANDY WITH THEIR MAULIES WHICH IS WHAT THEY CALL THEIR FISTS,
THEY TIE THEIR COLOURS TO THE STAKES BEFORE THEY START THE BOUT,
THEN THEY DOFF THEIR UPPER TOGGERY AND ALL THE PEOPLE SHOUT.....

HIT HIM ON THE BOKO, GIVE HIM POWDER, JOE,
POP HIM IN THE RATTLER, MAKE HIS CLARET FLOW,
LAND HIS RIBS A BENDER, TAP ANOTHER BIN,
DOUSE HIS BLOOMIN' DAYLIGHTS, THAT'S THE WAY TO WIN.

HIT HIM ON THE BOKO, DOT HIM ON THE SNITCH,
WHAT A PRETTY FIGHTER, WAS THERE EVER SICH?
NAFF HIM ON THE KISSER, CLOCK HIM ON THE DIAL,
SOCK HIM IN THE PEEPERS, CULLY THAT'S THE STYLE!

END NUMBER. (He collapses in the chair)

I sang that number after the boxing match between Heenan and King in 1863. I'd only been singing professionally for a couple of years. My first engagement, at the age of nineteen, was in my home town of Newcastle, at Balhambra's Music Hall, and from there I went down to Liverpool, to the Parthenon. I was using the name Joe Saunders then because my parents didn't want the family name of Leybourne bandied around the halls. I was billed as 'Mr Saunders, that characteristic comic vocalist and grotesque dancer.' I don't know why I bothered, changing my name that is. When I went back to being George Leybourne nobody could spell it right anyway. I was put down as Mr J Leyburn.... L-e-y-b-u-r-n.... Mr Laybourne spelt L-a-y. one advertisement the printer went completely cockeyed and had me appearing as Mr Seybourne. And you haven't heard it all. When I was at the Royal Cambridge, the Era billed me as Mr George.... wait for it... Geybourini! Geybourini? What did they think I was, an Italian high wire act? The Bedford was the first big hall I played in London, August 1863... and my reviews weren't exactly ecstatic.

PIANIST: Mr Labourne....

LEYBOURNE: Spelt with an A and no Y.

PIANIST: Is also among the company and vies for comic honours.

LEYBOURNE: Is that it?

(Pianist nods)

LEYBOURNE: Hmn.... Hardly the stuff to set the Thames alight. But, in 1870, when the Entr'acte published this cartoon of me.... *(He turns over the illustration on the easel to show the cartoon – UP IN A BALLOON)....* The English Lion Comique.... The editorial read...

PIANIST: It is about six years since we first noticed the lion comique at the West End Music Halls, and he appeared to us then a rather delicate animal.

LEYBOURNE: Huh! *(He goes behind the screen)*

PIANIST: Notwithstanding, season after season, his health strengthened together with his talent; and aided by the ever active and renowned agent, Mr Charles Roberts....

LEYBOURNE: Good old Charlie!

PIANIST: He soon established a reputation in all the principal halls and theatres of London and the provinces, enabling him to be amongst the very few artistes truly possessing public favour.

LEYBOURNE: Still the pet of London!

PIANIST: On our part we have to thank Mr George Leybourne for the many times he has given us pleasure whilst listening to 'Up in a Balloon', 'She Danced like a Fairy', 'The Bold Fisherman', etc., etc., etc.

LEYBOURNE: At the same time, a critic in the Ferret, a magazine of dubious wit, was calling my material....

PIANIST: The vile trash of his rubbish!

LEYBOURNE: Obviously I gave him no pleasure. Well, you can't please everyone. All you can do is try.

(By now he has changed into the costume for THE BOLD FISHERMAN)

THE BOLD FISHERMAN

THERE ONCE WAS A BOLD FISHERMAN,
WHO SAILED FORTH FROM BILLINGSGATE,
TO CATCH THE MILD BLOATER AND THE GAY MACKEREL,
WHEN HE ARROVE OF PIMLICO,
THE WIND IT DID BEGIN TO BLOW,
AND HIS LITTLE BOAT IT WIBBLE WOBBLED SO,
THAT SLICK OVERBOARD HE FELL.

ALL AMONG THE CONGER EELS, AND DOVER SOLES,
AND KIPPERED HERRINGS, AND THE DUTCH PLAICE,
AND THE WHITEBAIT, AND THE BLACK BAIT, AND

THE TICKLE BATS, AND THE BRICKBATS.....

DINKLE DOODLE DUM, DINKLE DOODLE DUM,
THAT'S THE HIGHLY INTERESTING SONG HE SUNG,
DINKLE DOODLE DUM, DINKLE DOODLE DUM,
OH, THE BOLD FISHERMAN!

HE WRIGGLED AND THEN HE STRIGGLED,
IN THE WATER SO BRINY,
HE BELLOWED, AND HE YELLOWED,
OUT FOR HELP BUT IN VAIN.
THEN DOWN DID HE GENTLY GLIDE,
TO THE BOTTOM OF THE SILV'RY TIDE
BUT PREVIOUSLY TO THAT HE CRIED,
'FAREWELL MARY JANE.'

ON ARRIVING AT THE TERRA FIRMA AT THE BOTTOM OF THE AQUA PURA, HE TOOK A COUGH LOZENGE AND MURMURED...

DINKLE DOODLE DUM, DINKLE DOODLE DUM,
THAT'S THE REFRAIN OF THE GENTLE SONG HE SUNG,
DINKLE DOODLE DUM, DINKLE DOODLE DUM,
SAID THE BOLD FISHERMAN.

HIS GHOST WALKED THAT NIGHT,
TO THE BEDSIDE OF MARY JANE,
WHEN HE TOLD HER HOW DEAD HE WAS,
THEN SAYS SHE, 'I'LL GO MAD,'
'FOR SINCE MY LOVE IS DEAD,' SAID SHE,
'ALL JOY FROM ME IS FLED,' SAID SHE,
'I'LL GO A RAVING LUNIAC,' SAID SHE,
AND SHE WENT VERY BAD.

WHEREUPON SHE TORE HER BEST CHIGION TO SMITHEREENS, DANCED THE CAN-CAN ON TOP OF THE WATER BUTT, JOINED THE WOMEN'S RIGHTS ASSOCIATION AND FREQUENTLY EDIFIES THE ANGELIC MEMBERS BY SOFTLY CHANTING....

DINKLE DOODLE DUM, DINKLE DOODLE DUM,

THAT'S THE KIND OF SOUL INSPIRING STRAIN SHE SUNG,
DINKLE DOODLE DUM, DINKLE DOODLE DUM,
OH, THE BOLD FISHERMAN!

DINKLE DOODLE DUM, DINKLE DOODLE DUM,
THAT'S THE KIND OF SOUL INSPIRING STRAIN SHE SUNG,
DINKLE DOODLE DUM, DINKLE DOODLE DUM,
OH, THE BOLD FISHERMAN!

END NUMBER. (He goes behind the screen to change)

PIANIST: *(Picks up paper and reads)* Mr Editor – Scarborough bathing – as a newcomer to this fashionable watering place, I have been startled at the shocking indecency practised on the beaches. Men are allowed to bathe in a state of nudity, which upon a very gradually sloping beach, leaves the bather barely depth of water to cover his knees. I have myself heard the man who takes the bathing machines repeatedly request a bather not to expose his er.... person.... and finally, requesting him to turn his back towards the beach. This was certainly a choice of evils. Many ladies are now deterred from riding on the beach in consequence of this nuisance, though some are seen driving at the water's edge, upon whose taste not the most complimentary remarks are made. It is surprising that those who have visited Scarborough for many seasons with their families should not have cried out against this evil. Let us hope sir, that as the great public organ of this land you will make your voice heard suggestive of remedy. Faithfully yours – no – moraliser.

(Leybourne steps out from behind the screen)

THE BIG HEAVY SWELL OF THE SEA

AS YOU MAY SUPPOSE WHEN YOU LOOK AT MY CLOTHES,
I'M PRINCE OF ALL NAUTICAL SWELLS,
AND THE FELLOWS I MEET TAKE A VERY BACK SEAT,
WHENEVER I FLIRT WITH THE BELLES,
NO MARQUIS OR EARL STANDS A CHANCE WITH A GIRL,
WHEN IN COMPETITION WITH ME,
IT IS ALWAYS SO, BECAUSE DON'T YOU KNOW,
I'M THE BIG HEAVY SWELL OF THE SEA.

THE FELLOWS LOOK UPON ME WITH A JEALOUS EYE,
THE LADIES ALL ADORE ME AS I SAUNTER BY,
THEY TITTER AND THEY BLUSH, THEN AFTER ME THEY RUSH,
FOR HEAVIEST OF HEAVY SEASIDE SWELLS AM I.

I TALK OF MY YACHT, MY CREW, AND WHATNOT,
MY YACHT'S JUST NOW UNDER REPAIR,
AND THAT'S BY THE WAY AND THE GOOD PEOPLE SAY,
I'M A DOUBLE DISTILLED MILLIONAIRE.
WHEN DOING THE GRAND TO THE STRAINS OF THE BAND
ESCORTED BY GIRLS TWO OR THREE,
I KNOW THERE'S A FEW, WHO'D THE SAME LIKE TO DO,
AS THE BIG HEAVY SWELL OF THE SEA.

THE FELLOWS LOOK UPON ME WITH A JEALOUS EYE,
THE LADIES ALL ADORE ME AS I SAUNTER BY,
THEY TITTER AND THEY BLUSH, THEN AFTER ME THEY RUSH,
FOR HEAVIEST OF HEAVY SEASIDE SWELLS AM I.

BUT WEEKS TWO OR THREE SEE AN END TO MY SPREE,
MY BILLS AS A RULE I DON'T PAY.
AND FLITTING IT DOWN, MEASURE RIBBONS IN TOWN
AND DINE UPON NINE PENCE A DAY.
SO IF YOU SHOULD POP INTO SOME DRAPER'S SHOP,

AND BE SERVED BY A FELLOW LIKE ME,
YOU'LL KNOW MORE OR LESS, THAT'S THE LONDON ADDRESS,
OF THE BIG HEAVY SWELL OF THE SEA.

THE FELLOWS LOOK UPON ME WITH A JEALOUS EYE,
THE LADIES ALL ADORE ME AS I SAUNTER BY,
THEY TITTER AND THEY BLUSH, THEN AFTER ME THEY RUSH,
FOR HEAVIEST OF HEAVY SEASIDE SWELLS AM I.

THE FELLOWS LOOK UPON ME WITH A JEALOUS EYE,
THE LADIES ALL ADORE ME AS I SAUNTER BY,
THEY TITTER AND THEY BLUSH, THEN AFTER ME THEY RUSH,
FOR HEAVIEST OF HEAVY SEASIDE SWELLS AM I.

THE HEAVIEST OF HEAVY SEASIDE SWELLS AM I.

END NUMBER.

Where was I? Oh, yes, not with the nudists of Scarborough but at the Bedford. After the Bedford I went straight down to the Oriental in Poplar. That later became the Queens, the hall where I was to make my very last appearance. Then to Brighton, name spelt wrong. Out to Manchester, three pounds a week and name spelt wrong. Oh, yes, appearing in London didn't mean staying put or being an overnight success, you know. From Manchester to Portsmouth. Hurrah for the Hampshire Telegraph! God bless the editor and all that print therein.... name spelt right! And, touring the country, Hull, Scarborough, back to Manchester, I knew if ever I was going to make the top league, I had to produce something special. But what? Well I trained as an engineer and I wasn't trained as an engineer for nothing. I invented a mechanical donkey. That's right, a mechanical donkey with a firecracker in it's tail. I named him 'Will-Ho' and, with him, I sang a number called the Donkey Rifle Corps. It did the trick. My Manchester engagement was extended from eight to eleven weeks and, at my benefit performance, not hundreds but thousands were unable to gain admission. I placed an advertisement in the Era saying I'd back my moke against any comic singer in the business, and Will-Ho's bray was heard in the far off metropolis. I was invited to appear on the bill arranged for the inaugural night of Mr Nugent's new London music hall, The Royal Cambridge – December 10th 1864. George Leybourne the inimitable on his mechanical donkey. The Cambridge engagement led to others and soon I was working three halls a night; the Cambridge, the Regent, and the Metropolitan. Then Collins was added to the list. And now, though I didn't realise it at the time, there came the most important moment in my whole career, if not my whole life. At Sam Collins music hall on Islington Green I met Alfred Lee and, together, we wrote a little number called 'Champagne Charlie'. I tried it out latter that year in Glasgow. Now there are some pretty rough towns and some pretty rough halls. At the Queens, Poplar, if the audience didn't like you they let you know it with a barrage of pease puddings, pork pies and pigs trotters. But, if you went down well in Glasgow, you went down well anywhere. And Champagne Charlie was not exactly a roaring success. The old favourites still worked; Mousetrap Man, Flying Trapeze, audiences never seem to get tired of them. But Champagne Charlie just ambled along. I must have sung well over two hundred songs in my career, some of them had to be also rans. It was beginning to look as if Champagne Charlie wouldn't even limp home. And then, I don't know how it started, but suddenly the whole world seemed to be singing or whistling

Champagne Charlie. You heard it everywhere. Such was it's success, that the Great Vance tried to go one better with a champagne song of his own, and Walter Laburnam threw out a challenge, 'I, Laburnam the London Lion Comique, am ready to sing against George Leybourne from five to fifty pounds – where and when he pleases in London.' Well, I wasn't in London, I was in Leeds, and I saw no reason to take up Mr Laburnam's challenge.

(He flips over the illustration on the easel to show the cover of SWEET ISABELLA and he goes behind the screen.

The pianist takes up a paper and reads.)

PIANIST: Princess Concert Hall, Leeds.... The star of Mr George Leybourne is still in the ascendant here and his popularity seems certainly to be as great as ever. He took his farewell benefit last evening when the house was crowded to suffocation. Leybourne is an artiste of extraordinary ability, and when once he has been seen, the exertions of would be rivals appear flat, stale and unprofitable.

SWEET ISABELLA

LEYBOURNE:
I LOVE SWEET ISABELLA, SHE LOVES ANOTHER FELLOW,
I OFTEN USED TO TELL HER, AND STAMP MY UMBRELLA,
IF WITH ANOTHER I CAUGHT HER I'D FROM THIS WORLD TRANSPORT HER,
HER LIFE WOULD BE MUCH SHORTER THAN SUN ON A RAINY DAY.
I LONGED FOR HER MY WIFE TO BE, THRO' GOING TO PARIS IT WASN'T TO BE
FOR WHEN SHE SAT ON THE FRENCH MAN'S KNEE, IT WASN'T THE CHEESE FOR ME.

OH SWEET ISABELLA, HER VOICE SO SWEET AND MELLOW,
I CAUGHT HER WITH A FELLOW THEN WITH MY UMBRELLA
I FETCHED HIM SUCH A SMELLER, AND KNOCKED HIM DOWN THE CELLAR,
BECAUSE SHE LOVED THIS FELLOW, AND SHE WOULD NOT BELONG TO ME.

ISABELLA YOU COULDN'T RESIST HER, JUST HERE SHE RAISED A BLISTER,
WHEN ONCE FOR HOURS I MISSED HER, AND KNEW THE FRENCHMAN KISSED HER
ONE DAY SHE THOUGHT ME SLEEPING, NOT ME FOR I WAS PEEPING,
AND SAW MY FOREIGN BROTHER WITH HIS ARM AROUND HER WAIST.
MY BLOOD WAS UP THEN WITH ONE BLOW, DOWN THE CELLAR STEPS I LAID HIM LOW.
WHEN SHE WITH HER HANDS SOON LET ME KNOW, SHE LOVED HIM BETTER THAN ME.

AH, YES.

OH SWEET ISABELLA, HER VOICE SO SWEET AND MELLOW,
I CAUGHT HER WITH A FELLOW THEN WITH MY UMBRELLA
I FETCHED HIM SUCH A SMELLER, AND KNOCKED HIM DOWN THE CELLAR,
BECAUSE SHE LOVED THIS FELLOW, AND SHE WOULD NOT BELONG TO ME.

BECAUSE SHE LOVED THIS FELLOW, AND SHE WOULD NOT BELONG TO ME.

END NUMBER.

PIANIST: *(Taking a copy of PUNCH)* A draft act of parliament by Punch... Every individual smoking outside an omnibus, sticking large pins in his cravat, wearing fierce studs stuck in his shirt, walking with others four abreast in Regent Street, reading slang publications, and adopting their language, playing billiards in public rooms, sporting dingy white gloves in the slips of theatres, frequenting night taverns, and being on terms of familiarity with the singers and waiters, thinking great things of champagne, as if everything at a party depended on it; and, especially, wearing the hat on one side, be the signal of most unmitigated gents, and shunned equally with hydrophobia.

LEYBOURNE: *(Over the top of the screen)* What did Punch leave out of that description of the smart man about town?

PIANIST: Not much. But, if you're referring to the really heavy swell, you add the tight trousers, the gold toothpick and little crutch stick which gave them the title of the 'Crutch and Toothpick Brigade' of which Vance sang....

HOW DO YOU LIKE LONDON? HOW DO YOU LIKE THE TOWN?
HOW DO YOU LIKE THE STRAND, NOW TEMPLE BAR'S PULLED DOWN?
HOW DO YOU LIKE THE LA-DI-DA, THE TOOTHPICK AND THE CRUTCH.....
HOW DID YOU GET THOSE TROUSERS ON, AND DID THEY HURT YOU MUCH?

(LEYBOURNE appears from behind the screen)

THE COMET OF THE WEST

LEYBOURNE:
I'M THE COMET OF THE WEST,
IN THE SHADE I PUT THE REST,
ALL OTHERS ARE MY SATELLITES YOU SEE,

BUT MOONING'S NOT MY GAME
I'VE WON MY WAY TO FAME
AND THEY ALL HAVE TO STAND ASIDE FOR ME.

SHOUT, BOYS, SHOUT AND LET'S BE JOLLY,
STAND ASIDE AND LET THIS SWELL GO PAST.....
I LIKE TO DO THE GRAND WITH A SHORT CANE IN MY HAND,
FOR, BY JOVE, YOU SEE THE COMET'S COME AT LAST.

IN BELGRAVIA I SHINE,
WITH THIS TAKING WAY OF MINE,
AND IF IN ROTTEN ROW I CHANCE TO RIDE,
MY HORSE HOLDS UP HIS HEAD
AS THOUGH HE PROUDLY SAID,
'THE COMET COMES! YOU FELLOWS STAND ASIDE.'

SHOUT, BOYS, SHOUT AND LET'S BE JOLLY,
STAND ASIDE AND LET THIS SWELL GO PAST.....
I LIKE TO DO THE GRAND WITH A SHORT CANE IN MY HAND,
FOR, BY JOVE, YOU SEE THE COMET'S COME AT LAST.

THOUGH OTHER STARS MAY FALL,
I SHINE BRIGHTER THAN THEM ALL,
AND THE COMET'S SHINING SPLENDOUR IS ITS PRIDE,
YOUR APPLAUSE THEN KINDLY LEND
FOR MY TALE IS AT AN END
FOR THE COMET OF THE WEST COME STAND ASIDE.

SHOUT, BOYS, SHOUT AND LET'S BE JOLLY,
STAND ASIDE AND LET THIS SWELL GO PAST.....
I LIKE TO DO THE GRAND WITH A SHORT CANE IN MY HAND,
FOR, BY JOVE, YOU SEE THE COMET'S COME AT LAST.

SHOUT, BOYS, SHOUT AND LET'S BE JOLLY,
STAND ASIDE AND LET THIS SWELL GO PAST.....
I LIKE TO DO THE GRAND WITH A SHORT CANE IN MY HAND,
FOR, BY JOVE, YOU SEE THE COMET'S COME AT LAST.

FOR, BY JOVE, YOU SEE THE COMET'S COME AT LAST.

END NUMBER

> So, in 1868, William Holland, known as 'The People's Caterer', engaged me for a full year at the Canterbury at the stupendous salary of thirty pounds a week. I bumped that up to near a hundred and twenty by appearing at other halls at the same time. Not a bad screw for the period when you consider the average middle class income was three hundred pounds a year, and that of the working classes, twenty pounds a year. Holland also insisted I live it up in style, cut a dash, and I obliged. Why not? It was champagne, champagne, champagne all round, and the best of cigars. And no more riding in cabs. Oh no! I now had my very own coach and four, complete with tiger.... that's the lad on the back, and coachmen dressed as jockeys.

THE UPPER TEN

LIKE FAM'D JACK BRAG THAT DASHING BLADE
WHO LIVED IN BYGONE DAYS,
DISGUSTED WITH MY FATHER'S TRADE,
MYSELF I SOUGHT TO RAISE,
HIGH IN THE FASHION OF THIS WORLD,'
SO WHEN MY DAD DIED, THEN
I SPENT THE CASH HE'D EARNED BY WORK
AMONG THE UPPER TEN.

WHEN I BELONGED TO THE UPPER TEN, THE UPPER TEN, THE UPPER TEN,
SUCH GLORIOUS WOMEN AND HANDSOME MEN,
WE SWELLS OF THE UPPER TEN THOUSAND.

(Seque into)

WHO'S COMING OUT FOR A MIDNIGHT RAMBLE

WHO'S COMING OUT FOR A MIDNIGHT RAMBLE,
WHO'S COMING OUT FOR A JOLLY GOOD SPREE,
I'LL BE THE ORGAN, YOU TURN THE HANDLE,
I'LL STAND EXS'S COME WITH ME.

I'LL BE THE ORGAN, YOU TURN THE HANDLE,
I'LL STAND EXS'S COME WITH ME.

END NUMBER

Oh, they were good days, good days. How could they last?

(PIANIST plays an echo of AFTER THE OPERA)

Laburnam the Longitudinal soon put paid to the coach and four. He hadn't forgiven me for not rising to his challenge so he took to guying me by driving around in a cart pulled by four white donkeys with his coachman wearing a shoeblack's cap. Everyone saw the joke, including me, so my own coach went. But others arrived. When I was appearing at the Oxford, Oxford Street, on either side, from the Circus to Tottenham Court Road, was lined with private carriages. Society had discovered the music hall. Leybourne was at the top of the ladder. A part was especially written for me in a pantomime at the Surrey Theatre.... Mephistopheles... and I was invited to play in a cricket match, South of the River artistes versus North of the River. I played for the South and made... five runs, before I was caught and bowled. They said, if I hadn't spent so much time in the refreshment tent and, when on the field, had kept my eye on the ball instead of the girls, I might have notched up a decent score. Well, it was only fun wasn't it? It was all fun. It was meant to be. They said I was blue. They said I was vulgar. It's not easy staying on top of the ladder when people are taking pot shots at you. It's for your own good, George. You're too generous George. You're too lavish, George. You're too fast, George. I hear you had a row with your agent, George, he's taking you to court. Your benefit was a shambles; half the people advertised to appear didn't and the other half said they hadn't been asked anyway. Go away, George, go on tour. By the time you get to town the fuss will have died down. George Leybourne is a cheat! He held a song contest for amateurs and then sang one of his own songs as the winner. Letters to the Era... accusations... counter accusations, go away George, go out on tour. By the time you get back the fuss will have died down. And you're still as popular as ever, George. You still pack 'em in. You can still get work, and it's champagne all round!

(PIANIST starts to play, very quietly, TING TING)

On a foggy winter's evening a stranger might easily miss the old Queen's Theatre in Poplar. It lurks in the High Street, yet belongs as the whole neighbourhood does, when the fog has swallowed up everything but the little islands of visibility around each scanty lamp-post to a gas-lit, bygone, tumbledown, London.

TING, TING, THAT'S HOW THE BELL GOES,
TING, TING, A PRETTY YOUNG THING...

Of course it's long disappeared, the old Queens. Long, long disappeared. So have they all. The old Parthy in Liverpool, one of my first and one of my favourites. Oswald Stoll took it over when his step father died. Oswald was fourteen at the time, managing the hall for his mother. The last time I played the Parthenon, one week in 1883... one night I failed to turn up at the theatre. Oswald came to look for me at my lodgings. He found me slumped in a chair, in no fit state for anything... *(Sounds of audience)...* 'Please come, Mr Leybourne, your friends are waiting for you.' 'Friends? Friends? I have no friends. It's my friends who have brought me to this.' Fourteen years old he was, but he got me to the theatre.

THE PRINCE OF PARADISE (Reprise)

AND I WAS THE PRINCE OF PARADISE,
I WAS THE PRINCE OF PARADISE,
EVERY ONE LOVELY, EVERY THING NICE,
JUST THE PLACE FOR ME, DEAR BOYS.

(He stands for a moment and then turns to go behind the screen, singing softly to himself, a tired old man)

AWAY WENT MY DREAM OF PARADISE,
'TWAS BUT A DREAM MY PARADISE,
EVERYONE LOVELY, EVERYTHING NICE,
TOO GOOD TO BE TRUE FOR ME.

END NUMBER.

PIANIST: The summer of 1884 was one of the hottest on record. According to the Birmingham Daily Mail of August 12th, the shade temperature in London reached ninety two degrees and in Birmingham, in the sun, a hundred and twenty eight. From various parts of the country deaths from sunstroke were reported. After the Queens Theatre, Poplar, in July, George Leybourne was booked to appear that August in Gatti's and the Hungerford. He did not appear. His place at Gatti's was taken by Mr Charles Coburn, and at the Hungerford, by his daughter Florrie. On the 15th September 1884, at his home in Englefield Road, Islington, George Leybourne died at the age of forty two. Doctor Humby, who signed the death certificate, gave the cause of death as exhaustion and abscess of the liver. The Comet had burnt itself out. When it was revealed that he had died almost penniless a benefit was immediately arranged for his widow. For Leybourne was not only the most popular singer of his time, but a great favourite amongst his brethren. He was buried in Abney Park Cemetery, Stoke Newington, and in the same grave are buried his daughter, Florrie, his son in law, Albert Chavalier, and their son, Frederick, aged twenty two. Cost for the extra depth, six shillings and sixpence.

(LIGHTS GO DOWN and COME UP to reveal Champagne Charlie in costume and pose)

CHAMPAGNE CHARLIE

I'VE SEEN A DEAL OF GAIETY THROUGHOUT MY NOISY LIFE,
WITH ALL MY GRAND ACCOMPLISHMENTS I NE'ER COULD GET A WIFE,
THE THING I MOST EXCEL IN IS THE P.R.F.G. GAME,
A NOISE ALL NIGHT, IN BED ALL DAY, AND SWIMMING IN CHAMPAGNE.

FOR CHAMPAGNE CHARLIE IS MY NAME,
CHAMPAGNE CHARLIE IS MY NAME,
GOOD FOR ANY GAME AT NIGHT, MY BOYS,
GOOD FOR ANY GAME AT NIGHT, MY BOYS,
CHAMPAGNE CHARLIE IS MY NAME,
CHAMPAGNE CHARLIE IS MY NAME,
GOOD FOR ANY GAME AT NIGHT, BOYS,
WHO'LL COME AND JOIN ME IN A SPREE.

FROM COFFEE AND FROM SUPPER ROOMS, FROM POPLAR TO PALL MALL,
THE GIRLS ON SEEING ME EXCLAIM 'OH WHAT A CHAMPAGNE SWELL!'
WHOEVER DRINKS AT MY EXPENSE ARE TREATED ALL THE SAME,

FROM DUKES AND LORDS TO CAB MEN DOWN, I MAKE
THEM DRINK CHAMPAGNE.

FOR CHAMPAGNE CHARLIE IS MY NAME,
CHAMPAGNE CHARLIE IS MY NAME,
GOOD FOR ANY GAME AT NIGHT, MY BOYS,
GOOD FOR ANY GAME AT NIGHT, MY BOYS,
CHAMPAGNE CHARLIE IS MY NAME,
CHAMPAGNE CHARLIE IS MY NAME,
GOOD FOR ANY GAME AT NIGHT, BOYS,
WHO'LL COME AND JOIN ME IN A SPREE.

GOOD FOR ANY GAME AT NIGHT, BOYS,
YES, CHAMPAGNE CHARLIE IS MY NAME.

At the end of the number the champagne bottle explodes sending a shower of glitter as the LIGHTS SNAP TO BLACK OUT.

www.ingramcontent.com/pod-product-compliance
Lightning Source LLC
Chambersburg PA
CBHW020023050426
42450CB00005B/619